Grace Revealed
Bringing Joy to the World

James E. McReynolds
Minister of Joy to the World

Parson's Porch Books

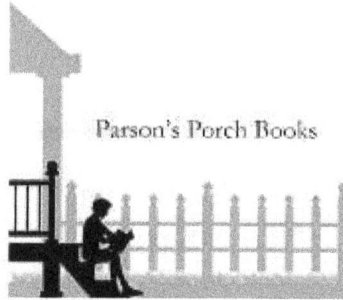

Grace Revealed: Bringing Joy to the World
ISBN: Softcover 978-1-955581-94-3
Copyright © 2022 by James E. McReynolds

Parson's Porch Books is an imprint of Parson's Porch *&* Company (PP*&*C) in Cleveland, Tennessee. PP*&*C is a self-funded charity which earns money by publishing books of noted authors, representing all genres. Its face and voice is **David Russell Tullock** (dtullock@parsonsporch.com).

Parson's Porch *&* Company *turns books into bread & milk* by sharing its profits with the poor.

www.parsonsporch.com

Grace Revealed

Contents

Dedication

To all my Mennonite friends with whom I have been privileged to share in the National Mennonite Health Assembly and in peace- graced congregations in the Midwest and in the United Kingdom, where in love and grace, the Mennonite Church, USA has given me hope and by amazing grace brings in the peaceable reign of God Shalom.

Foreword

James McReynolds is one incredible human being. It is hard to believe that any human mind could brim so constantly with wonderful thoughts and ideas. Every book that Jim writes seems to bristle with countless brilliant observations and quotable quotes.

Each volume is a great big, gorgeous bonfire burning in the dark of night and emitting sparks in every direction, suddenly and often illuminating the landscape and revealing things the reader had never imagined.

When I learned that Jim had written this book about grace, I had trouble believing he had done it. Grace is such a hackneyed subject in most Christians' experience. Every minister I know has preached sermon after sermon on the topic, almost always without saying anything new or fresh about it. What could this author possibly say about it now that hasn't been said thousands of times before?

I should have known better. Jim has amazed me with almost every book he has written. His mind is an incredible reservoir of facts and ideas that invariably seem to shatter the night with their incredible freshness and brilliance.

Chapter after chapter, he offers pungent remarks and illustrations to illustrate an old, familiar subject, and to leave the reader shaking his or her head and saying, "Wow! That is brilliant! or, "That is something I never thought of!"

In my day, I was a preacher too, like Jim, and I'm sure that through the years I preached some sermons on the subject of God's amazing grace. But I am also sure that none of those sermons—not one of them—contained the wealth of ideas and illustrations that are the hallmark of these chapters in Jim's book. I have often thought, while reading the manuscript of this book, how great it would have been, all those years ago, to have had this book as a resource I could have turned to before attempting to write my own sermons. I know my sermons would have been better if I had.

So, preachers, be sure this volume is on your shelves now. You will turn to it often over the years and be thankful you have it. It will enrich every effort you make to share the wonderful grace of God with your needy congregation.

Dr. John R. Killinger Warrenton, Virginia

Introduction

I have always believed in guardian angels. About a month ago, my wife and I were traveling to the county seat to renew my driver's license. We stopped at a dangerous and busy crossing with a red flashing light and a stop sign.

As we looked, there was a stopped semi facing us on the other side. I had been waiting for it to complete the trucker's turn into the highway.

I looked again and another truck was speeding down the left side. I quickly braked as my guardian angel appeared to say, "Stop."

In God's grace, the angel saved us. It is not whether it was God saving us in grace, or God's angel. As a child and today as an adult, I have prayed for my personal angel to stand with me, and to travel with me wherever I go.

Preaching a series of sermons on angelology, I heard stories about angels from God's guiding people. I have had numerous experiences that I could share. More and more people claim to have seen or experienced the presence of angels. Marilyn Webber has studied angels as much as I have studied joy. Her husband Bill did research on angels during his Ph.D. studies at Midwestern Baptist Theological Seminary in Kansas City, Missouri.

I connect my security, hope, light, and protection with angels. Angels are messengers of hope. Matthew 18:10.

My lifetime of studies on joy caused me to realize the importance of emotional nuance. I am an INFJ personality type, so Inner Nuances Foster Journeys. Nuances matter as we try to explain experiences. In my calling as a preacher, a teacher, a writer, and a licensed psychotherapist, I depend on the grace of God. The ability to name emotions and explain experiences is essential.

Brene Brown wrote, "So often, when we feel lost, adrift in our lives, our first instinct is to look out into the distance to find the nearest shore, that solid ground, is within us. The anchor we are searching for is connection, and that connection is internal. To form meaningful connections with others, we must first connect with ourselves, but to do either, we must first establish a common connection of the language of emotion and human experience." (Brene Brown, *Atlas of the Heart*, p. xxx)

We need to be loved unconditionally. We want our love returned. When it is, joy streams from our faces. Love brings life to people whose hearts have turned into stone. When we become love, we love everything around us. We view the setting sun with love. The love of God streams into us.

People have always connected love with angels. When we experience somebody's love, we say they are an angel. We feel that an angel has come into our lives. Love is a mystery bubbling up in us. We do not create love by ourselves. We can't see love or grab hold of it. We often do not know how to accept love. We are afraid to express love to others. Old or young, pauper or prince, we yearn to love and be loved.

I know that believing in angels brings difficulty. Angels exist to serve God with grace resulting in peace. Angels are created by God. They never age nor will they ever die. I have read thousands of stories about human experiences involving angels. For a trustful authority on angels, there is nothing better than Holy Scripture. We read of the actions of angels in the Word of God. Angels are messengers who make announcements. Luke 1:26, 2:8. Angels bring comfort. Acts

27:23-24. Angels heal. Job 33:21-24. Angels communicate. Zachariah 1:9. Angels give guidance and direction. Acts 8:21.

We find records of hundreds of actions by angels in the Bible. This book is not a volume about angelology. As we ponder these stories, we wonder about the possibility that we have entertained angels "unawares."

Grace gives exuberance as sparkling liveliness. Our words spew out of us. This experience is natural for children. When we grow older, we yearn to live life like that again.

We want to settle down in comfort. Living in this world, we have no permanent home. We move on. We leave things behind. Grace enables us to leave the old life. We must continue to unpack our tents. The unknown causes us to become anxious and afraid.

We need hope for existing in this time and place. We leave eternal blocks. We open doors. God's grace and peace gives us new ways of living. It gives us courage to go on. We go with strength. We travel with initiation into the mysteries of grace.

We get an inkling that our lives are becoming completely whole. We are fulfilled. Grace puts back together what has been torn apart. Grace completes us in what is in the fragments. Love investigates us like a telescope. Sin looks through a microscope. So long as a person loves, she or he forgive.

Humility is essential for comprehension of what grace is all about. Because of the grace of God, we act with courage to face all the truths about ourselves. We can judge nobody else.

All human beings bend down and realize their earthiness. With humility we are filled with humor. In our grace and peace, love and joy, we become able to laugh at ourselves. Humility is a strange thing. When we think we have attained it, we have lost it.

We are human beings with weaknesses and faults. God has also created us to be loveable. The tragedy of life is not that women and men perish, but that they cease to love. God and the beloved angels create space around us in which all creation steps into holy reality which is the family of heaven. That is how God graces the world with joy.

Mother Teresa of Calcutta told us, "I have found the paradox that if I love until it hurts, then there is no hurt, but only more love." The world is graced with beauty when our hearts are filled with love.

God's purposes for implanting signs of constant love draws us closer. We delight in being more like God. We feel like a surfer on the waves of grace. With every book I write, I seek to unfold the mystery of God's common grace.

When we fulfill that ultimate quest, we know that the grace of love is being and doing. Ultimate commitment brings ultimate love. Matthew 5:44-45. Glorious grace calls us to be closer. We know excitement and joy as the privilege to help carry God's ways while we live on earth.

Grace is so common and regular. Common grace is the stage for unbelievably great things. When we attend a musical concert, we look at all the people arriving. Anticipation of something wonderful makes us anxious for the show to begin.

Read Jude 1:1. Jude's small letter contains a triad. He says we are called, beloved, and kept. Jude highlighted the grace that is personal for believers. We are kept in God's love for the sake of Christ. We are transferred into a prized status of belonging with God in Christ. Jude 1:3. This gift is ours also.

Yearning monks and adventurers in far-off places stay in touch with God and the special journey.

We share salvation. We are one body. The faith content we know merits our highest devotion. No religion or any sect has spiritual insight that increases, supersedes, or supplants what God has already given. We are to be merciful to those who have doubted. Jude 1:24.

Jude was addressing people who had a calling. That does include us. This book was written to shed light on someone's path. Any reader who finds his or her wings will be lifted to an illumined place where there is no darkness.

This inner journey through dark entanglements of our existence into pure love.

Chapter One
Grace as Everyday Miracle

Grace is everywhere, like lenses that are not noticed as we look through them. God has given us eyes to notice grace every day.

Grace gives us strength to do things we otherwise could not do. This happens as a result of being in an intimate relationship with God. The more intimate we are to God, the more time we spend in a quiet place with God. Power from God come as a direct result of abiding in God's presence and being connected in a meaningful way.

I believe our loving God graces us with angels that are never far away. I have enjoyed the fun of loving people. Now I am having fun as an author.

Awake or asleep, I feel the brush of angel's wings. Writing is how I share the grace of joy. Recently, I did speech therapy because of a weakness in my throat. Doctors feared that there was a tumor in my larynx that could silence my preaching and teaching. God is gracing me with healing.

At any moment, the gift of grace is available. Grace in God is the loving tendency of the divine to pity the miserable, to bless the unworthy, and to pardon the guilty. God is the God of all grace. The grace of God is the foundation for salvation. It is the hidden spring from which flows every good and perfect gift. Grace has no borders. It has no limits. God's grace has no boundaries. It gives forgiveness. God's grace has no bounds. It offers humble souls eternal security. The grace of God has no barriers. It can be received into every soul. God's grace has no end. It is available for the asking.
The gospel is called "the glad tidings of the grace of God." Scripture tells us grace is for sinners. Grace is to be received and enjoyed.

My wife and I enjoyed a performance before 2,600 people with Celtic Woman, an international group of musicians, at the Orpheum Theater in Omaha. Toward the end of the show, they sang "Amazing Grace." Silence hovered over the crowd. In the silence, the crowd's senses were enhanced. Grace turns up the volume on our senses. Amazing spiritual energy brought joyful tears to many eyes.

Every person's conversion is unique. There is something about this hymn that is relatable to people everywhere. In 1922, the hymn was recorded by the Original Sacred Harp Choir. It was sung by Rosetta Tharpe, J.M. Gates, and Aunt Molly Jackson. During the Civil Rights Movement, activist Fannie Lou Hamer led protesters in singing "Amazing Grace." The mass singings helped in defining racial equality as a spiritual and moral pursuit.

Since 1772, the year John Newton wrote the hymn, grace seekers remember when and where they first believed. Ironically, this stirring song, closely associated with the African American community, was written by a former slave owner. In 1972, Judy Collins' recording of it, began 67 consecutive weeks on the music charts.

Aretha Franklin, Ray Charles, Johnny Cash, Dolly Parton, Willie Nelson, Elvis Presley, and thousands of others recorded "Amazing Grace." It has appeared on more than 15,000 albums.

John Newton's beliefs had lacked conviction. Newton's life was rife with the "dangers, toils, and snares" at which the text suggests. He was brought face-to-face with the thought that he had been miraculously spared. He had numerous near-death experiences. Nevertheless, Newton quickly went back to his old habits. (Steve Turner, "Amazing Grace: The Story of America's Most Beloved Song," pp. 1-54)

"Amazing Grace" is a hymn that is recognizable to almost every American, regardless of religious background. No wonder the crowd at the Orpheum Theater in Omaha were entranced when the ensemble of Celtic Woman shared this hopeful hymn.

Grace is not well understood. Several people who wrote books on grace used the title *Grace Is Not a Blue Eyed Blonde*. We need the grace of God. Read Ephesians 2:1-3. This book is a symbol of my own graces. Grace blessed me with a grace-filled daughter. Her mother was named Nancy Grace. Her grandmother was named Grace.

Grace is an everyday miracle. Grace happens. Grace fills our families with joy unspeakable and full of glory. God's grace is the heart and soul of faith. Grace is God's gift to you.

Thanking God for our food is hardly said at mealtimes. I like, "Gracious God, for this meal and those who made it, and for those around this table sharing it, we are thankful." And from a Cherokee friend, "Great Spirit, we give thanks for the living beings, the animals and plants, that gave themselves for our meal. We give thanks to all who eat with us."

Here is one from a Midwest farmer, "Blessed is the Earth for providing our food. Blessed is the sun for nurturing its growth. Blessed is the wind for carrying the seeds. And blessed is the rain for watering them." A college student prays,

"Beloved Mother Nature, benefactress of all, you are here on our table as food. Give us the strength and wisdom to help us share it with all of our brothers and sisters."

Grace period is a limited time to pay monthly bills without paying a penalty. When we accept the abundant love and have the courage to die to fear and control, we let Christ through our gate. Graceful dancing is needed in the church. We become the grace margin in the graceless world. Eric Law, Inclusion: Making Room for Grace, p. 11)

The Holy Spirit challenges us to walk in the grace of God every day. Grace reminds us of the character of God. Grace and mercy are tied together. Mercy is not getting what we deserve. Grace may feel passive. There is active strength required to obtain grace. Getting grace requires action. We must be willing to accept God's grace. Knowing that we can never deserve grace requires action. We must stop trying to earn grace.

Acting and not striving are active processes. Waiting in the grace of God is not passive. A weak person will not live by grace. Grace requires us to accept grace daily. We allow God to change us. We allow grace to mature through practice. We release the need to control. We gain understanding of divine grace. We spend more time with God in intimate prayer and Bible study. We live openly in the community of the body of Christ.

Justification means God has covered our sin. God does not see us in all our sinning. God gives grace when life is going great. God gives more grace when we are in the pits. God's grace is not what we do. It is all about Jesus and what he did for us.

Grace is forgiving. It frees us from sin. It is never earned. It is about having faith in Christ. There is no cost to you. Jesus paid the full price.

Sanctification is concerning walking with God, staying open, and allowing God to change us to be more like God. Allowing change requires the strength of the Lord.

Both justification and sanctification refer to a change God is working in us. This beautiful transformation requires our willing cooperation. We are stuck when we refuse grace. Fighting grace is to fight change. God changes us with divine grace. Read I Corinthians 15:10. God fills us with the Holy Spirit of grace.

Marianne Williamson was one of the presidential candidates in 2020. In her recent book, she explores the ways and means to nourish the soul in our harsh world. (Marianne Williamson, *Everyday Grace: Having Hope, Finding Forgiveness, and Making Miracles*, 366 pages)

We see that the gift of grace gives us power to live life as a Christian. We must accept the grace of God by accepting grace every single day. We extend grace to others. God does not think less of us for asking for grace. Our need for grace will not take grace from needier others. Embrace God's grace instead of attempting to prove our worthiness. It is difficult to receive love that is not earned. With grace our desires change. Connection with God brings a realignment.

Old loves no longer thrill. We are new and different persons. We become what we love again and again. The pleasures of this world are more delicious in the larger context of the love of God. Physical beauty, glory, the sweetness of music, the fresh smell of flowers, and perfumes. That is what we love when we love God.

Grace is a spiritual gift for our receiving grace. Grace is a spiritual gift. It will mature over time, when it is used and accepted. Grace means that beautiful things are being done for us. Grace is transformative, constant and beautiful. By grace, we become more like Jesus, to be a person who loves better and sin less. Grace is not only evident in the help God gives us, but in the pleasures and grace. There pleasures include beautiful sunsets, little children laughing, a great tasting tea or coffee, or the joy of people in love.

Grace is all these things, big and small. Grace is real and practical. The radical beauty of grace is unmerited and unconditional. Because of grace, God's unthinkable love for us, we experience all these forms of grace and more. Take time to appreciate and notice all these differing graces. Be thankful for the saving grace of Jesus. Notice all the many ways the Holy Spirit is with us every day. Look for ways grace works in us through sanctification and conviction.

Enjoy the beauty of nature. Let all things leads us to Jesus to remind us how amazing grace really is. And together now and in heaven, we will sing with new meaning, "Amazing grace, how sweet the sound that saved a wretch like me. I once was lost, but now I'm found, was blind, but now I see."

Grace gives us an overflowing supply of mercy. It never runs out. It is abundant.

There are many faces to God's grace. Embrace each one. There are many faces we must encounter. Grace is beautiful. It gives hope and love from God above. It is strength when we feel faint. It is praise. It is adoration. It is amazing.

Grace showcases the glory of God.

We share in grace by faith and by faith alone. Grace pardons the guilty and the shamed. Jesus took the brunt of our disgrace. Grace softens, remakes us, restores, and reforms us.

To God be the glory, great things God has done.

Chapter Two
Grace as Life-Sustaining Water

Our hearts, minds, and souls are thirsting for life sustaining water. Everything that lives needs water. Grace offers supernatural water. Read John 7:37-39. Water is fascinating.

Lake water or the vast ocean reflects the golden sun, dark clouds, large trees, and differing things. When we become still and patient so we can listen to the water as it speaks to us.

Water is not only a source of beauty with shades of blue, green, and gray, but it is a place for nature lovers. Water brings life.

Water can cause suffering and pain. Many thousands of people have lost their lives in the waves of water. Towns have been swept away by extreme floods.

The symbolism of water motifs has connotations for Christian baptism. The natural purifying effect becomes a symbol of spiritual cleansing.

The threatening forces of water evoke connotations of death and the grave. Thousands of military personnel have been buried in the ocean. Water also symbolizes the renewal of life.

Crossing the Red Sea and the Jordan River signify the journey as the Israelites left their lives of slavery for the graces in the Promised Land.

These events could not have happened without water. Creation and salvation are bound together.

When we examine the practice of baptism, we observe that baptism is a human witness, obedience to the example of Jesus, and a promise to keep a clear conscience before God.

Christians say together with the apostle Paul that "we have been buried with him by baptism into death, so that, just as Christ was raised from the dead by the glory of the Father, so we walk in the newness of life. Romans 6:4. Water baptism is said to be a mere symbol pointed toward something bigger and more important. Many people in the pews value it as an actual element of God's grace.

In the ancient world and in third world nations today, water in a precious commodity. Lack of rain makes the catching and saving rainwater important. Water signifies the reception of the Holy Spirit. Water is a symbol for the Holy Spirit coming into a person's life and cleansing the soul from sin.

Holy Scriptures inform us that water is a symbol of the day of the Messiah. John 7:37-39. Jesus told a woman in Samaria that he is the one who gives living water to hose who have a spiritual thirst. John 4:14.

Jesus gives life-giving water to those who believe. This water is eternal life by the grace of God.

Because rainwater is absolutely necessary for survival, rain represented satisfaction and prosperity. Without the Spirit of God, none of us could have spiritual satisfaction. Isaiah 41:18. The prophet is saying the Messiah will bring water to the barren places of the desert.

Water has a number of important symbolic meanings for the believer. In the dry and desert world of the Bible, water was so important as a symbol of the work of te Holy Spirit.
The free grace of God is the water of life. Read Revelation 22:1. Revelation is grace revealed. This book has three parts: the things which John saw the things which are, and the things that shall be. Life and grace are often found together. Jesus himself

spoke to a sinful woman about drinking "living water." Read John 4:10. Jesus spoke of "a well of water springing up into everlasting life." To be without Christ is to be without life. John shows Christ is the one giving living water. In chapter seven Christ is the fountain to satisfy the thirsty.

"Water of life" is the blessed grace of God that gives eternal life. Like the river in Eden was to water the garden, so living sustaining water is a blessing of grace. The joy of the church will be drinking of living water, ever unfolded to us. Our souls will forever rejoice will a fullness of joy.

Let us look are where the water of life comes from in its origin "proceeding out of the throne of God and of the Lamb." God is the God of grace, and Jesus Christ is full of grace.

We must first drink living water before it can spring up into us. This living water flows from us. The grace of God brings salvation.

When Paul and the apostles wrote, they usually started by writing, "Grace unto you and peace, from God the Father, and from the Lord Jesus Christ."

John Chrysostom preached, "When the grace of the Holy Spirit enters a soul and is established there, it gushes forth more powerfully than any other spring. It never ceases, dries up, nor is exhausted. The inexhaustible gift of grace is gushing water to indicate its force. Read Isaiah 12:3.

Jesus came to give us the living, life sustaining water of grace through the Holy Spirit to bring healing to our souls. The Spirit fills us with overflowing. We then spill out the love of God and grace onto those living around us. Let us bless the grace of water. Water gives grace to a river falling toward an unseen ocean. Bless the humility of water. It is willing to shape itself to the otherness that holds it.

Water has been used in blessings Water stands between earth and fire. Water is usually odorless and colorless. Our human bodies are 80 per cent water. Water is use in the sacraments to confer transformation.

Stand under fountains of grace. Pursue the resources of grace. Get wet. Remember that nobody in the Bible complained about the parting of the waters of the Red Sea.

Grace is like water entering empty spaces. Consider the showers of blessing. Quiet spirits are enabled to see beyond the present, to focus on the invisible as God's ways are higher than our ways.

Paul understood the abundant grace of God in a personal way. Read Ephesians 2:4-9. The grace of God was granted to Paul while he was "yet sinning" as a Pharisee who persecuted Christians. Out of his overwhelming experience of grace, he became an apostle. He took the gospel far beyond his Jewish community into the world of the Gentiles. This passage from Paul's letter captures his understanding of the essence of grace. Paul is teaching to respond to amazing grace by leaving behind our preoccupation with scarcity and self- preservation and moving to extend our boundaries by sharing grace with others.

Grace gives us a time and place for our exploration. In grace we listen to the Holy Spirit to empower us, to inspire us. Working in grace is a worthy thing to do, independent of the outcome of our exploration.

Ministering in this grace-filled way, we shall learn how to imitate Jesus by bending down and writing on the ground, allowing time for constructive questioning, reflection, and self-examination. Read Ephesians 4:25-5:2.

Grace is the place where there are flowing streams. "Tis grace that taught my heart to fear and grace my fears relieved; how precious did that grace appear the hour I first believed."

As the lovely blue-eyed blonde Celtic Woman sang "Amazing Grace" before thousands in Omaha, the soprano had the audience in her hands. Believers began to retrieve last memories for the words they had heard before in other places.

"When we've been there ten thousand years, bright shining as the sun, we've no less days to sing God's praise than when we first begun."

An epiphany happened that night, and we saw the power of God descending on us that night. I know. The world thirsts for grace. When grace comes, the world falls before it.

An old story tells of a man who died and was met by Saint Peter at the gate of heaven. "Before I let you in let me ask you some vital questions about going to church, giving your ten per cent, and being graceful with others." The man assured Peter that he had done these things and more. Finally, the man said, "The only way I can get into heaven is by the grace of God." Saint Peter then opened the gates.

Grace in God sustains. If God was not gracious, humankind would have no hope. Grace from God comprises every good thing that is bestowed on us sinners. Grace is sustaining water for those who cannot merit or deserve the grace that supplies needs, makes humans alive from the dead, cleanses us from pollution, protects the defenseless, supplies the needy, and crowns God with everlasting glory.

The grace that the gospel presents includes all the sustaining water needed, received, and enjoyed. God will give showers of blessings to any who will receive it. Grace blots out sins, renews the soul, disperses doubts, and saves us freely, fully, and forever.

The is abundant grace for all times. None of us know what is before us. Times and seasons change. There are times of darkness and times of light, times of conflict and peace, times of trial and times of triumph, times of health and times of illness. Grace sustains us in all circumstances. The water of life sustains us in all places.

The God of grace is with us, the throne of grace is before us. The promise of grace sustains us. Grace in each of us is just a drop in the ocean. Feel the sustaining water in the ocean of grace. Read II Corinthians 9:8-9. Nothing is impossible with God. God makes grace abound in us. Our God brings joy unspeakable and full of glory. Grace remains faithful, blessing us with visible signs of invisible grace.

Life can change in a few seconds. We need our angel, protection, and grace. We look back on life just an hour before, it seems far away. Imagine someone's life has now changed permanently, irrevocably. We never know what destiny will shape our lives.

Nobody is disqualified because they are unattractive. All lives are crooked. Sin makes us ugly. If grace depended on our own integrity, goodness, or sincerity, there would be no hope. In all times and in all things, grace pours water on us. Read Philippians 4:13. My grandmother Betty always said, "God never puts you where grace cannot keep you." Grace is the strength of God. "The joy of the Lord is my strength."

God continues to give us all we need. Look around you. Life is full of extravagance and prodigal graces. Streams of mercy never ceasing call for songs of loving praise.

Grace that cannot be seen is not the grace of God. People are not interested in our professions of faith. They are impressed by what we are and do. Actions speak louder than words. It is better to live a holy life than to just talk about it.

Living now in my eighties, I do wish I knew what I know now. I have come to realize that the desire to be perfect, as well as expecting others to be perfect, are marks of a deeper anxiety. I know now that there is nothing sacred or holy about trying to be perfect. Too much damage has been done by imposing this expectation on the people of God.

Like the joy of the water of the sea coming home to shore, may the relief of grace rinse your soul. As water takes whatever shape it is in, so free we are to become to be.

The grace of liberation was given to me when in seminary, where I read the texts about perfection as a poor interpretation of what is in the word of God. "Perfect" does not mean moral perfection. It describes completeness or living an undivided life. To be a whole person the inner life is aligned with the outer life. The call to wholeness is a call to integrity. Jesus wants us to live life holistically. The inner life is in harmony with the outer life. We stand on holy ground. We discover what a flourishing life looks like and feels.

Jesus was a healer of the soul. Jesus knew what our souls long for. He knew what calls us to life. He knew what souls crave. We were born to be whole. Jesus does not expect us to be perfect, but whole, one, and complete. We are not called to be perfect, but to be passionate for the kingdom of God to come.

Scripture tells us that God finishes what God starts. Read Philippians 1:6. Grace will sustain you. Sustaining grace is the power to keep on going when we feel like giving up. Sustaining grace will keep us standing when we face temptation. Read I Corinthians 10:13 and I Peter 5:8. If we get tired, grace will keep us standing. Read II Corinthians 1:21-22. When we are troubled, grace will sustain and become our refuge and strength.

To receive God's sustaining grace, we call out for the help of God. Read James 4:6-8. We revive when our minds are filled by the Word of God. We receive support from the people of God. Read Galatians 6:2. We receive the promises for strength to soar on wings like eagles. For older folks, they will walk and not faint.

Chapter Three
Grace as All Things All the Time

Time is something we do not control. In our culture of affluence, time, wisdom, and friendship decrease. Read Matthew 6:31-34. "The time is being fulfilled and the Light shall shine, just when it appears to us that the darkness is impenetrable," Eberhard Arnold said. Read Luke 2:5-6.

We can only wait, yearning in the darkness with fervency as we long for the holy proclamation that will bring about the fullness of time.

In the gospel of John, Jesus is in Bethany at Simon's house with Mary and Martha. Grace has made it possible, because Lazarus had been buried in a tomb. It was a joy to all. Mary pours an expensive perfume over Jesus' feet and body.

Like a bath and body works store, the entire house is filled with the fragrant perfume.

Judas wondered why Mary would do this thing. And why was Jesus so receptive? Smells form memories. The sense of smell elicits lasting memories. Mary's action was a gracious thing of one so indebted and devoted to another. Mary had learned from Jesus the ways of God, the ways of love and grace. This time Mary demonstrates her wonder and gratitude. She was forever changed by Jesus. We are never the same once we are covered in fragrant perfume of the grace of God. The smell stays with us, filling our lives until we just cannot carry the memory with us.

Did this smell stay with Jesus? For how much time did it linger? Jesus kept smelling the perfume as he entered Jerusalem, during his final meal with his disciples, as he hung on the cross, and said, "It is finished."

Mary had done the right thing. It had cost her so much.

We do not realize the impact we have on others. Every time I see my dad's hat, it is just like he is here with me again.

We do not realize how deeply the actions of our lives are taken in by another. In every encounter, we have the opportunity to share our feelings, our thoughts, our graces.

Grace leads us to a joy that is in all things all the time. All things work together for good in making the love of God known, as we are living testimonies of the grace that fills the world. Like a precious perfume, it fills the earth, stirring within us the goodness of God.

Grace means we are forever loved. The sweet smell of grace calls us back toward future that is promised. Love, joy, and grace abounds in and through our lives in everything and in every encounter.

Seeing all things as grace corrects our vision. Grace is an ophthalmological corrective working on the eyes of our souls. When we focus on the outer appearance of things, we are not able to see as God intended. Pray to God to "open the eyes of our hearts," so we can see Jesus. We can see all things with this perception. Grace helps us see all things through gospel eyes. When we listen to world news, heaven is the vision. Grace works all things together according to the counsel of the will of God.

Grace changes our focus as we look at flowers, trees, mountains, stars, oceans, and sunsets and sunrises, all flora and fauna, and even weather patterns in terms of the purpose of God. Heal our spiritual eyes to help me see into the things of God.

Grace sees pain and suffering with mature eyes. Most of the time, we want to hide, deny, or run. Grace has ultimate compassion for things we cannot understand. The grace of God is boundless and powerful. Grace is rich and valuable beyond our feeble understanding. God sees us as valuable because of what it cost. It is valuable for the things it offers. It brings complete provision of all our needs. Grace is to abound beyond measure.

Read Ephesians 1:7 and 2:7 to see what the riches of grace are.

Grace gives complete redemption and complete forgiveness. It gives inexpressible kindness of God through Christ Jesus. In abounding grace, God thrusts kindness toward humankind in al things, including the cross.

The riches of the grace of God includes the finished work of Christ. Read Hebrews 10:10-14. It includes the convicting work of the Holy Spirit. John 16:7-11. It is the saving work of God. Titus 3:7. The riches of the keeping work of God. John 10:27-30.

By grace God deals with us not on our merit. God does not act on what we all deserve. Instead, grace responds to us on the basis on God's goodness and generosity. Grace makes it possible for all people in all times to experience salvation.

Grace supplies us with an innumerable amount of underserved favor in everything and in every day of our lives.

The grace of God is far beyond our ability to totally comprehend. It is invaluable to the entire human race in all things in all time.

The problem with organizing our time is that time has so many crosscurrents of events. Time belongs to God. We are stewards of time. We are responsible for every minute God graces us with. On the eve of preaching a sermon, I feel I might have prepared my message in too much of a hurry. I rush to get it done.

We work in differing rhythms. I never had a typing lesson. Somehow, I write volumes with just one finger. I can write all day once I am inspired or passionate about something. Other writers are amazed.

God exists outside of time. God created time as an artist chooses a medium to work with, but the Creator is not bound by it. God sees the past and the future as an eternal present. When God looks at my life graph, God sees not the jagged swerves toward good and toward bad. The goodness of Jesus captures in a moment of time applied for all eternity.

Christians begin all time from Christ's coming into the world. Christmas is a new beginning. The birth of Christ is a gift in time that causes us to know that all is not simply in flux. The entire time of the world is a short span of human life that holds a rhythm. This recollection of the Christian reckoning of time since the birth of Jesus draws us to the creation of the earth, which is our origin.

Christian people are those who are continually looking at the beginning of something new. If God can begin something with humankind because humans do not use God's time as a method of calculation, then a true era begins. Since the birth of Jesus, time has been filled and fulfilled.

Grace appears in many forms. Grace means there is nothing we can do to make God loves us more. Grace means that God already loves us as much as an infinite God can possibly love. Grace existed before we ever came to be. Grace is God's part. Faith is the positive response to what God already provided. Faith is our part. Grace and faith work together. Ephesians 2:8-9. We are saved by grace through faith, not one or the other. Grace is what God does. Faith is what we do.

Salvation does not depend on grace alone. God's grace is the same toward every human being. Titus 2:11. The sins of the entire world have been forgiven through Christ Jesus. John 1:29, 16:8-9. God's grace has provided for our salvation and for every need of our lives.

Faith appropriates what God has provided. Faith does not move God. Faith does not cause God to do anything. Faith and grace work together. Our part is to accept what God has already done. Grace must be balanced with faith.

In much of our teaching and preaching, God is misrepresented. The idea that God either causes or allows evil so that we will somehow grow spiritually is not true.

Peter wrote about "the God of all grace." Grace is unfair. Some find it difficult to swallow. Grace is not always reasonable. The gospel of grace begins and ends with forgiveness. Whenever I hear anyone sing, "Amazing Grace," I realize that grace is the only thing in the universe that has power to break the chains that enslaved generations in every era or time.

Grace has never been easy. Few find it forever satisfying. God forgives my sins as I forgive others their sins against me.

Our Lord is ready and waiting for us. God refreshes us. Look at all things all the time and know the majesty of God. Consider three verses from the Bible: Jeremiah 31:25, Isaiah 40:29, and Acts 3:19. May your spirit be refreshed by the grace of God. Joy changes us. Joy is found in simple things, but it happens in time and place. On special occasions, I buy roses and other flowers for my wife. Flowers always brighten her spirit. One time, the prettiest flowers were droopy. They quickly wilted. Knowing the joy of the Lord is much deeper than the cheerfulness of a temporary flower.

Faith conquers discouragement, opening the way for genuine, surprising gladness. Remember how God gave gracefully in past times. Rejoice in God's faithfulness in the present time. Trust God in the future.

Joy comes from God, not from changeable people or unstable circumstances. Whenever we receive the gifts of the fruit of the Spirit, we enjoy a quiet confidence of faith that is supported with joy. Grace is a quiet light shining in every soul. Without it, our days would be wearisome and empty. The word grace strikes a sense of warmth and protection.

Nobody's life is alone and unreachable. Grace evokes a privileged intimacy. Human souls plead with the divine. Our times are desperate for belonging. In the grace light, we are illuminated in a unique way.

Temporary joy fills a moment but reflecting on the joy of the Lord is more satisfying. As C.S Lewis knew, differing stimuli trigger desire in differing people. (C.S. Lewis, *The Pilgrim's Regress*, pp. 9-15)

Our culture gives us many cues about how to live inside time. We are told to spend it. We use words that we use in financial matters. Spend. Save. Manage.

Christmas time is waiting. God waits and we wait. God's being like us is not limited by taking on feet, hair, and a body. Christmas is waiting for God. For centuries people have waited for God to come. Waiting as God is born. Expecting peace. Waiting for God to come back. It is in time when we enter God's waiting.

Time continues to go on. Grace means we hone our skills of being joyfully present now. We wait for all things that have already happened, and for something that has not occurred yet. Read Psalm 74: 12-17.

We need not wait for God to light a fire. Waiting might be desired if God lights the fire. We would just stand around and bask in glow, the warmth, its love and power. God has already lit the fire. God did not give us a spirit of intimacy. The embers keep burning inside us. The fire waits to be restarted.

We sing in conference and camp setting, "It only takes a spark to get a fire going." During summer camps, leaders spark fires for evening gatherings. Those camp guides spark a fire quickly with their experience and practice. They can begin a full-fledged bonfire that lasts through the night.

The next morning a camp advisor walked over to the fire pit, crouched down over an ash pile that had burned out. He began to dig into the ash and blow. He said, "The fire is not dead yet. We can get the embers to spark and before we know it, the fire will be back to full force."

Some focus on the end time or the second coming of Christ. Paul and others thought they were living in the end time. Jesus would come in their own lifetime. Focusing on the end time is like an embarrassing relative, still present in our home. Despite the expectations of early Christians, the second coming has not happened.

Many just ignore the theme. Not every church community is comfortable ignoring the end times theology.

The theme is preached by many sermons, studies, and published book such as the Left Behind Series. Ignoring it is not a solution. Removing traces of end time theology from our discussion makes a nonsense of our hymns and the themes from the Bible.

We do have a vision of the end times. Our times include the end time. The time is between the beginning of the end and the end. Waiting for the future includes a vision of what the world has potential of being. Future waiting collapses time, just as waiting for the past. The concept is mind blowing. We fail to grasp it in its fullness in this time of earth. Grappling with this is part of what God invites to do. This grace leads to contentment and joy.

The world is troubled everywhere. Wars rage in too many locations to count. The church is conflicted and fractured. Relationships falter. Hopes are dashed. Dreams appear too foolish to speak about. Credit runs out. Families disappoint. Destinations are not reached. Pets must be put to sleep. Gunfire never stops. Faith does not sustain us.

Paul tells us to "stir the flames of faith" in his advice to Timothy. It is meant as a survival technique. The word can also mean "to kindle." To kindle means "to start a fire, rouse, inflame, or light up."

This instruction to kindle the gift of God that is within us. The apostles asked Jesus "to increase their faith." Jesus answered by talking about "having faith as a mustard seed."

"Rekindle the gift of God that is in us." We think it is failure in faith that prevents us from getting where we need to do. We think our broken, insufficient, compromised faith needs to be strengthened, restored, defended to connect with God. Faith is a gift. We kindle the faith that is already within us. That is why we keep on gathering to rekindle the grace of the gift of faith.

When time is short, life becomes urgent. Things become simplified. The brevity of time causes us to pray and watch. It is amazing how things come into place. Time is short. Prayer keeps us calm, doing things in time for the glory of God.

The nature of calendar time is linear. Its duration begins and ends. Beneath time there is an eternal depth. This mysterious fact offers us a different way of relating to time. Spirit unfolds the intimacy of time. Eternal life is eternal memory. We can now imagine a place beyond endings.

Grace has given us differing personalities, different gifts, unique responsibilities, individual expectations, unpredictable behavior, and new hope. Grace is usually unexpected. The benefits are surprising.

We live in a world that is not our home. We are pilgrims on a journey in another land. When we are weak in faith, joy strengthens us. No matter how dark the clouds are, no matter the size of hailstones pounding us in our homes, the sun will piece the darkness and hang a rainbow in the sky. Grace defies explanation.

As we get older, time slips through our fingers like water. We strain at the erosion of life. We journey on with no map. Nobody else lives life the way you do. We were dreamed of long before we were born. We walk on pathways never anticipated. It has become a relief for me to find my calling as a writer that expresses my spirit. When we find that what we are doing what we love, it makes for a rich and contented life. Our energy is immediate. Our passion is clear. We see what we do as the beauty of our soul.

Chapter Four
Grace as Abundance

Grace is a divine spark which ascends. With wings of grace, we mount up as eagles. Believers are citizens of heaven. Grace humbles and elevates. Grace gives a double perfume. Grace gives a fragrance to holy things.

Victor Hugo tells the story of Jean Valjean. *Les Misérables* is a story of abundant grace. Valjean has been released from hard time in prison for stealing bread. He had to carry an identity card. For days he walked the village roads, seeking shelter when he was graced by a bishop. While living in the bishop's home, he could not resist the temptation to steal valuable silver. He left in the darkness.

Early the next morning, three policemen knocked on the door of the bishop. They had Valjean in chains. They had caught him with the bishop's silver.

Grace in abundance was displayed, as the bishop cried to Valjean, "So, here you are. I am delighted to see you. Had you forgotten that I gave you these silver candlesticks as well. These are silver like the rest. These are worth 200 francs. You forgot to take them."

He then told the police, "Valjean is no thief. All this silver was my gift to him."

The bishop's grace defied every human instinct. Valjean kept the silver to remind him of abundant grace.

Accepting grace removes every issue from a purely personal human endeavor and places them in the realm of God. It removes us from a need to be powerful or right. Grace is turning to God and seeing how God through Christ mediates, appreciates, and embraces sharing the abundance of grace.

Richard of Chichester wrote the words of this spiritual hymn in the year 1200: "Day by day, O dear Lord three things I pray: To see thee more clearly, love three more dearly, and follow thee more nearly day by day." (Eric Law, *Inclusion: Making Room for Grace*, p. 81)

Living in abundance appears like a myth. It will never be attained. To move from being not enough to being more than enough, we receive this special grace of God. This means that the grace of God will overflow so we will have more than enough to meet our needs. God wants us to be a blessing by receiving grace for abundance. Read I John 4:7-16.

Reader, we have been walking a spiritual labyrinth on our journey toward living abundantly. As we walk toward the center, we are seeking to be transformed. As we continue to move outward, we are seeking to transform.

Trusting God's grace and practicing spiritual disciplines help us continuing to turn the pages of faith. Faith leads toward enriched life, but not necessarily to riches. Evangelists who preach the power of consumerism preach in an environment of scarcity. Listen more to those who preach and write with words of abundance that fill the dry waters of our souls and the inner void that thirst for more.

Teaching abundance is difficult. There remains mistrust and fear for the future. Scarcity sells. The scarcity syndrome causes fear of others, so we buy many things. We have security devices, homes in safe neighborhoods, guns, and high- priced insurance.

Fear takes away our freedom. Fear gives society the power to manipulate us with promises and threats. The world is viewed as dangerous and sparse.

We continue to live as paupers though our inheritance of spirit is vast. We find joy in the journey filled with refinement and riches. Rewards and gifts become vital to who we are. Greeks believed that time had secret structure. Suddenly time opens and grace is revealed. Jews believed that time has its own seasons as is recorded in Ecclesiastes. Time is opened for surprises, exciting opportunities Abundance can bring joy to the world. Grace exceeds reason. Grace is the purest complexion of the soul. Grace is the flower of delight which Christ loves to smell. Grace is to our souls as the eyes to the body, as the sun to the earth, as a diamond to a ring.

Grace is forgiveness that forgets. It is favor in absence of merit. It is love that stoops. There is abundant grace for everyday sinners. Grace is not affected by the degree of sin. Grace salvaged "the chief of sinners." Grace salvaged publicans and moral delinquents.

Those whose names were written on police records would be written in heaven. Gospel teachers recognize that grace is powerful enough to reach the worst sinners.

Grace takes the smoker from cigarettes. It takes the addict from the needle. It takes the thief from the stolen loot. It takes the pornographer from websites. The gospel is for fragrant sinners. They can change. We must never use the excuse that we have lived in sin too long. Take a step with faith by grace and God will help us to finish the journey.

Grace is necessary for ordinary sinners. Most people do not see their need for grace. We do not have to feel lost to be lost.

Any sinner is lost. Being a good person does not erase sin. Being a nice person does not mean one will be saved.

God gives more grace as we need it. I Corinthians 5 speaks of an early church member who was guilty of scandalous sin. He had had a sexual relationship with his father's wife. Paul instructed the church to withdraw from him if he did not repent. He did not and they did.

Later, this sinful man came to his spiritual senses and repented. Paul wrote back to the church about God's grace and forgiveness, telling church members now to comfort him, and confirm their love toward him. II Corinthians 2:6-8.

The same welcome awaits us today. If we have wandered, we can choose to come back.

Grace teaches us to live soberly and righteously. Titus 2:11-13. Our secret sins require special grace. Secret sins are the sins we commit that other people do not know such as lust or hate. These sins are unknown to us and others but known to God. Some are sins of omission. Some secret sins others know we have committed that we have no memory of, such as offending somebody who never told us about it.

There is grace for young people. Youth have inexperience. They make mistakes. Some of these mistakes are sinful. The psalmist wrote, "Remember not the sins of my youth." Psalm 25:7.

Youth have the ability for enlisting, resisting, and persisting. Ecclesiastes 12:1.

There is sufficient grace for older people. The last days of life on earth bring concerns. Psalm 71:9. Grace is reassuring at this time. An aged Paul was confident as he wrote his final books. II Timothy 1:12.

Chapter Five
Grace as Mysterious Holiness

A magnificent mystery lies between the holy nature of God and grace that reaches us in our everyday lives. When we encounter light in darkness, we cover our eyes. The holiness of God is blinding. Read I Timothy 6:16.

Holy means "to separate." God is exalted above all things. Holiness is incomprehensible for our limited minds. Read Isaiah 6. God initiated an act of grace by reaching out to Isaiah with forgiveness. Only then could he stand in God's holy presence.

Read Zechariah 12:10. The cause of grace is the spirit of God is called "the Spirit of grace. The Spirit is the fountain where the crystal streams of grace flow. When my musical wife plays the harp, no sound comes out unless she touches the harp with her fingers.

God does not remain unapproachable. God is not off somewhere on a mountain far away. A magnificent mystery lies between the holy nature and grace for our God desires a personal reconnection with everyone of us. Extending grace comes where God's grace and our lives intersect. The Holy Spirit initiates transformation. Grace is such a magnificent mystery as our holy God chooses to restore relationship. When we begin to understand God's holiness, we shield our eyes spiritually from the brightness. I Timothy 6:16. God's holiness is almost incomprehensible to our limited minds. God is perfect and pure and deserving of our reverence. We decide how we will respond to God's holiness. We have sinned and are not worthy of being in the presence of God.

I Peter 1:13-21. What comes into your mind when you think of the holiness of God? How do verses 17-18 define the holiness of God? Verses 3-12 describe our salvation through Christ.

Readers, talk through these words about holiness together or preach a sermon on this text or teach it in a study group. Participants will know that they are holy in Christ in verse 18. They will set their mind on the hope of future grace when Christ returns in verse 13. Conforming our desires to Christ in verse 14. Finally in our fear and uncertainty, they choose holy conduct in verse 17.

God never casts us away because of anything we have not done or have done. God connects with us despite our undeserving condition.

God does not remain unapproachable. God desires personal reconnection by extending grace. By receiving that grace, we receive total forgiveness, complete acceptance, and unconditional love. The Holy Spirit initiates transformation in our receiving hearts. Only by God's initiative of extending grace to us can be enjoy such a relationship. Isaiah 57:15.

What a magnificent mystery! The exalted God of the universe chooses to restore the relationship.

We can wrestle with this mystery, and we can attempt to explain it. We struggle but God never casts us away. All we can do is to accept and receive it.

God is holy. God's grace is amazing.

The holiness of God fits us for communion and connection. God's grace keeps us in constant fellowship. We should desire grace above all things. Comfort is nice, but grace is much sweeter. Endeavor with zeal to place the jewel of grace into the cabinet of the soul. Grace has a soul-quickening excellency.

Dead things have no beauty. There remains no beauty in a dead flower. Grace is the vital artery of the soul. It is the light of life.

We are grafted into Christ the vine. We are made not only living but lively. Divine energy enters our souls. Faith is an enriching grace. It puts the serpent's eye in the dove's head. The riches of God sanctify other riches. The riches without grace hurt us. They are golden snares. They ignite the fuel of lust and the bellows of pride.

Grace sanctifies our riches. It corrects the poison. It takes away the curse. Grace brings satisfaction that any other riches can't do.

Grace fills up every space of the soul. Joy is a foretaste of heaven. God's grace puts beauty and luster upon a person who accepts it.

The smallest revelation is holy. It comes to us from a living God. The step toward the right direction is a step of faith made in response to grace. The coming of the Holy Spirit no longer must blow me away to have an effect. The Spirit reveals how we become a living witness to its message. This guided instruction Jesus called "born from above."

Most of us misinterpret this phrase by emphasizing the moment of birth rather than acknowledging the process that birth initiates. The birth of my daughter gave our family and friends great joy. The word birth implies growth. Our false interpretation leaves us as spiritual infants.

We never ask, "What is the least I can do and be a Christian?" The Spirit shows us to live as God intends us to live in our remaining days on earth. We separate membership from discipleship. We replace intake with outflow. We need to look at the way God wants to reveal what we must know at this time in our lives. This enables us to grow in grace.

In my work and calling as the Minister of Joy to the World for a lifetime, I have discerned the difference between people who have been traditioned and those who practice faith as free- lancing Christians. The difference lies in perspective, the sense of moving in a stream of wisdom that has been ebbing and flowing for an extended time. The difference is illustrated by a flower growing in a garden and a flower stuck in a vase. Each one looks he same. The one placed in a vase is dying. Becoming a cut flower, it lacks roots that keeps it alive.

Hugh Wamble, my first professor of church history at Midwestern Baptist Theological Seminary, introduced me to the Didache, which warned against false prophets who wandered from place to place, never rooting themselves with believers with whom they could share authority and accountability. John Wesley called cut-flower Christians "holy solitaries."

They were separated from the guidance of the counsel of members of the body of Christ. This guidance comes in differing forms. It is not selfish. It is specific. It is unique. Just as we have fingerprints, we have soul prints.

The unmistakable mark of a renewed mind is the sole desire for our lives to be instruments through which the will of God can be done on earth as it is in heaven.

God calls us to become servants who live with compassion and authenticity. "People care how much you know when they know how much you care." Love is the key. This love appears natural, rather than contrived or filled with secondary motives. People are sorry to see you go when it is time to leave.

The Holy Spirit guides us to the fruit of the Spirit. People remember these fruits long after they have forgotten the loving behavior.

Jerry Bridges said that he traveled throughout the world preaching on the pursuit of holiness. He emphasized how grace transforms and holiness follows. He took his sermon notes and published them in a book, Pursuit of Holiness. It sold five million copies. His second book, Transforming Grace sold more than four million copies.

Bridges said it is the grace of God that is the power enabling us to pursue holiness.

Chapter Six
Grace as Connection

Grace brings moments of bliss. During one of my vision quests, I shared how grace had brought joy into my life. I invited the audience to share some of their own stories. As people revealed their experiences, everyone felt moved and inspired and connected.

Nothing is more important than the formation of healthy relationships that establish deeper connection with people living around us. One of the tasks of life is freeing ourselves by widening our circle of compassion to embrace all of creation and its beauty.

I realized that just talking about grace makes people more open to its influence. We were all wrapped in a cloak of spiritual energy.

Unmistakable connections were made.

God created us with a deep need for connection. We need each other. An ember that lies outside a fire will soon die. When placed near the other embers, it keeps on burning. We warm up in God's graceful love.

Jesus took his closest friends when he prayed. Read Matthew 26:38. We are vulnerable, and we need help in the tough places. We need encouragement from our parents, our grandparents, and everyone to walk through the valley of life.

When my daughter was born in Nashville, Tennessee, I had never felt such love. I felt so blessed, so graced to be the parent of a little girl. Grace is my blue-eyed blonde.

One perspective on living is in connection to our community. Linda began her life journey with a disconnection. As a newborn, she was being shoved from the womb, having the umbilical cord cut.

A home connection makes us feel love and loving. Home is where we feel cared for. We are missed when we don't show up.

We long to be connected to God in a place where we know we belong to God. Some moments we feel the connection. A bush in our souls begins to burn with a fire of oneness with God and a connection with all there is. Purpose and meaning are inherent for our longing for belonging. Our own belonging is found not in excluding others but by including them. In a connecting community, we experience God's transforming love and begin to taste the meaning of living abundantly. (Marilyn Brown Oden, *Abundance: Joyful Living in Christ*, 7-16)

We connect with God with our senses. Amy Frykholm wrote about a seventy-century monk who died in exile named Maximus the Confessor. Monothelites argued that Jesus Christ was fully human and fully divine but had one divine will. If Jesus did not have a human will, then he could not serve as a full bridge between humans and God. Jesus was separate and other. Maximus was convinced that humans could be friends of God. He saw the incarnation as an invitation into an intimate connection.

The writings of Maximus are found in the *Philokalia*, a collection of spiritual texts that had influenced monks in the Eastern church.

He wrote about ways to unify bodily experience, rational thinking, and the work of the will so humans could connect in unity. Maximus believed that the physical senses corresponded to a "vivifying sense.

The sense of smell he connected to "an incensive faculty." Frykholm was mystified until she thought of the smells of a monastery she visited. Maximus wrote that smell leads to discernment and insight.

The sense of sight corresponds to the intellectual faculty, located in the human brain, which we translate as the mind. Our knowing connects specifically with seeing. The greater our capacity for sight defined as physical sight but also perception.

Hearing corresponds to the "rational faculty," the capacity to reason. Each act of listening is a spiritual journey. Listening to another human being or to a situation is a virtue, because as we listen, we clear distractions to hear as fully as possible what is being said. Love underscores true listening because it is never blown away. Reasoning is a connection to discernment.

Taste is the capacity for desire. Maximus named it the "appetitive faculty." Our desire, even the desire for food and water teaches us how God uses appetites to expand love. There is a connection between physical appetites and our spiritual appetites.

Maximus said the spiritual senses are connected to physical senses, but don't require them. Maximus understanding brings clarity and drama to ordinary living. Each of his "faculties" are connected. His vision is of the whole human being in relation to God, growing toward God like

a plant toward the sun. Maximus used the term "divinization," the slow transformation of our human existence into the image of the divine.

The spiritual senses tradition assets that God speaks through the tangible, sensible world. We connect to God with our capacity to delight. Spiritual and physical connection are what Jesus experienced in his own lifetime on earth.

Now consider how grace for people of disabilities who have limits on sensory perception have a capacity to develop keen sensations and perceptions far beyond the five senses. (Amy Frykholm, "The Five Spiritual Senses," Christianity Today, November 17, 2021, pp. 23-25)

Chapter Seven
Grace as Joy Unmistakable

Grace erupts at odd and surprising times. Grace is joy unmistakable overflowing of feelings of delight. Grace is a vibrant, fresh energy, the joy of life all around us. Suddenly, the vitality and immediacy of life itself are perceived in the flowers, in people, and in everything.

Grace causes us to be grateful. Intimacy with God is available all the time. Joy emerges in the simplest of life experiences. This quality of joy hangs around the edges, as we open ourselves to being awake with each encounter.

Joy wells up when we leave room in our consciousness for it to burst in bloom.

The indescribable grace of God was described by a story that happened during the American Revolutionary War. Peter Miller was a faithful preacher. He encountered a young man who demonstrated violence, evil, bad-mouthing Miller.

That young man was found guilty of treason. He was sentenced to death. Peter Miller set out on foot to the headquarters of General George Washington sixty miles away. George Washington heard the preacher, but emphatically said, "No, no, no. This man has been found guilty. I cannot grant your request for this friend of yours." Miller said he is not my friend. I have never had a worst enemy. Washington was amazed at the effort the preacher made for this man. Washington granted a pardon.

Miller then rushed to the place of execution. He arrived in time to see this man to the scaffold. Miller produced the pardon. The executioners saw the clear signature of President Washington and the life of his worst enemy was spared.

That was an unmistakable joy. Grace is necessary for the journey of life. Even when our destination is unknown, the joy of the Lord brings a new stability.

Read Psalm 16:11. There is unmistakable joy in God's presence. In grace, God knows our name. Read Isaiah 43:1. God will never forget us. By God's grace, the comfort of joy enters our hearts, and we feel closer to God. This joy gives us a new perspective. Grace and hope outlast any trial. We call to God. God hears us. Darkness seems so powerful.

We can look ahead to a time when rejoicing comes in the mourning. Read James 1:2-4. Joy in the Lord is our hidden strength. Grace helps us persevere when we think we cannot go one more step.

Paul was content when housed in a Roman prison. There he wrote the Joy letter. The Holy Spirit was Paul's source for contentment. Paul's unmistakable joy was connected with his position in Christ. The word grace implies divine grace. The fountain waters of Paul's joy were found not in this world, but in God.

Joy as the fruit of the Spirit endues even in suffering and hard times. Read I Thessalonians 1:6. I have studied joy in such places as Vanderbilt, Oxford, and Yale. I have preached hundreds of sermons about joy, taught the psychology of joy in many scholarly places. I find the most insight comes from sharing in the joy stories of ordinary people. The apostle Peter called joy "inexpressible and glorious."

The joy of the Spirit is set apart from all levels of human joy. Faith in God is required. Read Romans 15:13. Followers of Jesus are joyful people. Grace and joy change us. We will never be the same. Jesus as always full of joy. God anoints us with the oil of joy according to Psalm 45:7. Perhaps that was in his mind when Norman Vincent Peale anointed me as the minister of joy to the world.

Human joy flows from human love. When the love of God flows into our souls, we gain love for work, for people, and for life. When humans break down love, they destroy joy. No love equals no joy.

Nothing can diminish the flow of the sustaining waters of grace. Few know the spiritual sources of love, grace, and joy. The joy of the Lord is found in our assurance of salvation. The weight of the world is lifted from our shoulders when we know we are forgiven from our sins. Whenever we humbly accept Jesus into our lives, he brings inexpressible joy. Read Isaiah 61:10.

Joy relates to believing. Joy is making choices and creating habits. We create an atmosphere that makes joy come easily. Create a faithful habit. Eat, sleep, read, journal, pray. Say good morning to God. Create a special area in the home for a place to connect with God. Make it a quiet place. Let God speak to you. Also, prayer is how we speak to God. This form of communication is created just for us and God.

God works in the lives of the people who we have led to accept grace themselves. Joy is a product of the Holy Spirit. Joy is in the nature and character of God. The joy associated with the

Holy Spirit became a source of strength to rise above discouraging circumstances.

The presence of God is a source of joy. The disciples were overjoyed when they saw the Lord. Joy results when we read, live, obey, and meditate on the Word of God. Read Jeremiah 15:16. Praise and worship cause joy to spring up within us.

The many showers of blessing bring joy. Read Psalm 126:3. We rejoice as God supplies every need.

Praise and hopeful grace rush to my mind as I hear "Joy to the World" by Isaac Watts written in 1719. I found an old book in the University of Oxford's giant collections published by Edward Baines in 1800. Watts was a prolific pastor and writer of more than 700 hymns. Today it is a popular Christmas hymn, but it was not designed for Christmas.

The text of the hymn was first published in 1719.

Read Psalm 98. Those words inspired "Joy to the World." Neither the psalm nor the hymn says nothing about Jesus coming as a baby.

Watts' vision was to sing about God as King, the Messiah, who comes in glory and righteousness to comfort the faithful. We wait for the coming again of Jesus.

Watts' enormous volumes of sermons are also housed at Oxford. Watts was a preacher as well as a musician.

We sing to the Lord a new song. Psalm 98:1. We "repeat the sounding joy, repeat the sounding joy, repeat, repeat the sounding joy." The words were about the coming of Christ foretelling the consummation of all things to come.

When I visited Bethlehem several years ago, I stood in line at the Church of the Nativity to touch the spot where Jesus was born. Philips Brooks wrote, "O Little Town of Bethlehem," decades earlier as he stood in a similar line.

My human brain wondered if that was really the spot. One Israeli guide told us that Constantine, the emperor of Rome, made Christianity legally tolerated in 313 A.D. He sought to find relics and places associated with Jesus and the early church. When the emperor's mother found the spot of Jesus' birth, he built the Church of the Nativity on that spot.

I felt grace waves of joy. Joy is grounded in the reality of God's presence. When we feel joy, we are feeling God. Joy is a gift from God. We cannot create joy. In the Greek language, joy is built on the same root word for grace.

C.S. Lewis and J.R.R. Tolkien were professors at Magdalen College of the University of Oxford. They struggle with the meaning of grace and joy. They came up with the meaning of grace was that skeptical people can get close to God, and God will take over all other things.

We can quietly listen to "O Little Town of Bethlehem," and feel God's presence. Do you feel it? That is joy

Chapter Eight
Grace as Wonder of Christmas

Christmas brings the wonder of grace. Laying our heads down on Christmas night, we know we are under God's grace. Television commercials composed by car dealers proclaims, "Anybody can buy a car here." At the bottom of the screen we read, "With approved credit." That means we can buy a car if we meet the qualifications.

Today, Christmas is more than a holiday. Christmas is associated with our deepest longings. It is associated with dreaming about our loved ones and about going home. No other holiday is associated with magic. "He rules the world with truth and grace, and makes the nations prove the glories of his righteousness, and wonders of his love, and wonders of his love, and wonders, wonders of his love."

Read Philippians 2:6-11. Grace brings a glorious change in us as our desires and delight are fixed on heavenly things, instead of the sensual earthly things that draw us away from God and heaven.

Read I Peter 1:6-8 and John 16:8-15. With grace fix the eye of faith on the glorified Jesus. Our God of grace has convinced us of our sins in the days of our flesh. One day we in this time will behold the face of God.

We shall, be made like the angels, who are most active spirits and ministers of joy, who are flames of fire. Read John 17:1, 2-26.

Our hopes for Christmas are impossible. Given these expectations, some people feel let down when the season ends. They measure their experiences of the present by recollections of the past. Memories are idealized. Hopes for Christmas are deflated by discovering the stories of the magic that were made up or exaggerated. The wonder of Christmas has been forgotten. (Michael Patrick Barber, *The True Meaning of Christmas*, pp. 1-190)

Grief, illness, and ignorance are with us every night. Remember God and glory are at hand. Night is not known in heaven. Joy is the eternal emotion.

What if we remember together the wonder of Christmas? We would discover elusive contentment. We would be storing up treasures in heaven like Jesus told us. Our accumulated stuff would lose its grip. Read John 1:14.

Imagine the hushed excitement and the vivid anticipation of a child on Christmas eve. Anticipation was intense for those waiting in wonder. The grace of Christmas is the miracle of God entering into humanity in human form. Christmas causes us to enter joyfully into the realm of wonder. God gives us the authority on our own lives. (Hebrews 12:1-3)

The mood around us from getting up decorations to wrapping paper to music at the malls, and social gatherings bring on celebration. The weeks leading to Christmas are a frantic escape from wondering about the meaning. God made a benevolent invasion by sending a baby. God became utterly vulnerable. We follow God in Jesus, not because we have been beaten into submission, but because we have been loved back into the divine family. We need to quiet our minds, so we hear the word of God and see the face of God in our conversations and interactions with others. Families carry unique Christmas traditions from year to year and from generation to generation. (Edward Baines, *The Works of the Rev. Isaac Watts, D.D. in Seven Volumes*, Volume 7, pp. 8-78)

Give thanks for the traditions you observe from year to year. Be grateful for new experiences and new traditions you begin.

Love, grace, joy, and love. These words define Christmas. We show love by our actions. Each gift. Every ornament. All the preparation. Christmas is grace and love. Make a point to show appreciation for those in your family that are there for you.

Imagine the wonder of Christmas. Picture a family gathered together, a warm fire glowing in the fireplace. A wonderful Christmas may exist only in our imaginations. Our family includes people with flaws, faults, and frailties that do not disappear at the turn of the calendar.

Keep your eyes and ears open to see the needs and to hear the voices. Share with others the grace that God gives to you. Lean on God's unconditional love for you.

Think about your friends. We do thoughtful things for them. They respond by ding more thoughtful tings for you. With faithful friends, and even more with the grace of God, the love you give will come back to you.

People get much more than they deserve. God offers the grace of unmerited love. Grace comes to us as an art of being created. Renounce any idea that we can earn it.

Paul Tillich wrote: "Grace strikes us when we are in great pain and restlessness. It strikes us when we walk through the dark valley of a meaningless and empty life. It strikes us when our disgust for our own being, our indifference, our weakness, our hostility and our lack of direction and composure have become intolerable to us. It strikes us when, year after year, the longed-for perfection of life does not appear, when the old compulsions reign within us as they have for decades, when despair destroys all joy and courage.

Sometimes at that moment a wave of light breaks into our darkness and it is though, accepted by that which is greater a voice was saying, 'You are accepted. You are accepted by that which is greater than you, and the name of which you do not know. You do not ask for the name now. Perhaps you will find it later. Do not try to do anything now. Perhaps later you will do much more. Do not seek for anything. Do not perform anything. Do not intend anything. Simply accept the fact tat you are accepted.' If that happens to us, we experience grace. After such an experience we may not be better than before, and we may not believe more than before. But everything is transformed, changed. In that moment, grace conquers sin, and reconciliation bridges the gulf of estrangement. Nothing is demanded, no religious or moral or intellectual presupposition, nothing but acceptance." (Paul Tillich, *Shaking the Foundations*, pp. 131-132)

Think about the difference God has graced you with. Respond by making a difference in the lives of your loved ones and your friends. One person cannot change what is happening around the world.

Think about giving. Expect nothing in return. This graceful attitude brings grateful smiles. We never know whose life we touch.

Think about focusing on God and serving other people. By serving others without expecting anything in return, you and they will be surprised by joy.

The Spirit will open the eyes of your soul. Respond to others with joy, grace, and compassion, because you have experienced how God responds to you. Share the love of God by loving others in thought, word, and action. See how the more you give, the more you get.

We miss the essence of Jesus' birthday. Christmas is about God's coming to bring salvation. God may cause people to "wonder" as we share and really experience love and grace. People are open to hear about Christ Jesus during the Christmas season.

They have heard and even sung the Christmas hymns. They see houses decorated inside and out. Many have manger scenes. There are wondrous opportunities to tell others that the Savior of the world has been born. We can make it unmistakably clear to the unbelieving world that they wonder about the source of such joy.

Jesus prayed that we would become one with each other. Becoming one means what is good for us is good for all.

Christmas is a magical time. We can reflect on the graces of life. We can show our loved ones how much they mean to us. Families gather from big distances to exchange gifts. The joy and fulfillment found in these moments create eternal memories.

Christmas is the day that holds all time together. Each year Christmas comes and goes quickly. It fades with each passing commitment. While we dream about sitting down with our family in the living room to enjoy the beauty of Christmas music while gazing at the decorations. The wonder of Christmas comes as we dig deeper. Life has been marked by accumulation, ambition, and our version of success.

Angels told us that first Christmas that anybody could come to God. The wise men and the shepherds accepted God's grace trough the infant Jesus. They and we remember the good news of the birth of Jesus that has the power to bring us wonderful joy The joy does not depend on what is going on in our lives, the chaotic world, or the people we choose to be with.

No earthly thing can give us complete joy. The grace of God

brings the joy that still has power to overwhelm our souls with rejoicing. Unwrap this gift. Renew the awe and wonder of the miracles of the gift of Christmas.

Christmas is a perfect time to recapture the wonder of grace. Twinkling lights on a tree, sounds of joyful music, and the aroma of cookies baking in the oven create a calm atmosphere in our homes.

We spend hours decorating our home at Christmas. Our tree is decorated with ornaments from the places where we have been in the ministry of bringing joy to the world.

It is now July, but many of our decorations are still up. We see Jesus' best in our Christmas trees. Laurel has bought scores of manger scenes displays in cabinets for all to enjoy. When we view the lights, we know that Jesus is the light of the world. God uses these small things in life to express and point to the glory of God. Our family enjoys setting up nativity scenes. We use nativity scenes throughout advent.

We have control over how we celebrate. Christmas affects our souls, our families and friends. Who ever thought we were victims of Black Friday? We are not stuck spending more than we have. Christmas joy is not misguided by culture. Christmas grace allows reinventing rhythms, reclaiming its beauty, and restoring its delight. God gives free will, so we oversee how we accept life. We can focus on connection, love, generosity, and the coming of Jesus to bring joy to the world.

Join hands with the dearest people in your life and celebrate. God's grace gives us permission to leave the draining and exhausting parts of cultural Christmas. Grabbing onto its joy, its wonder, its magic. Jesus came in the simplest form to the simplest people and saved the world.
Ponder all that Jesus has done for all of us. Ponder God's

mercy. Ponder grace as God's love throughout the eras of time. Ponder. Ponder. Ponder. Let the pondering transport you to worship and adore our Lord.

Keep on pondering deeply all year long. As we experience temporal things, even life itself, we can ponder eternity.

We deeply desire serenity. The season of Christmas involves harried schedules of school and church activities, frantic buying and wrapping gifts. We run out of energy and time. Our wonder is how we can get everything done.

Children reflect the wonder in their eyes. They are amazed at the sounds, sights, and stories. As we grow older, the routines become work. If we are not careful, somewhere in between the amazement of a child and the work of pulling it off as adults, a sad thing happens. We lose the wonder of the season.

For children Christmas is a time of anticipation. For older people, it is a time of memory. Christmas is a bridge. Bridges are needed as the river of time flows past. God expects us to be generous with grace, time, and words. We are given room for surprises.

Looking into the Word from God, we can recapture the wonder of grace. God revealed grace to hopeless, hurting people through Jesus. God became one of us. God masterminded a plan for our redemption. God used the common trade language of koine Greek, so people could pass on the story of faith throughout the world.

Jesus was wrapped in our humanity. The gentleness of new life touches us as we hold a newborn. God came as a baby to soften our hearts to receive a transformed life that was offered to us in Jesus.

Jesus continues to be Emmanuel, God with us. God knew the

world needed a touch of grace. This dependent child of grace brings us the gift of eternal life.

During the time of the craziness of Christmas, we allow God to renew us. We come to God plain and unlovable, but we are made beautiful by grace.

Is this joyful faith an unmistakable possibility? Joy has been hard to discover with wars, shootings, the pandemic bringing sickness and death, inflation, loneliness, and new kinds of problems.

God dwells in joy, which is our strength. The Word of God, intimate praying, and gracious living give us joy. Joy overcomes sorrow The Holy Spirit restores the joy that is within all of us.

As we read the Psalms, joy appears 57 times and rejoice appears 43 other times. Joy and rejoicing appear during all our life experiences. Joyful faith pleases God. Joy continues to be my word. C.S. Lewis wrote, "Joy is the serious business of heaven."

As we look at the baby Jesus in a nativity set or in pictures in Christmas cards, keep in mind that we are adoring much more than a cute little child. Many church groups go out into their neighborhood singing carols. One of my great joys at Christmas is sharing the Word of God's grace and joy in nursing homes. Christmas carols contain Bible passages. This gives the singing power to touch the souls of people and to move us into a spirit of worship. May we never lose the wonder of Christmas. As the night falls Christmas eve, a spell is woven, childhood memories spring to mind, and the world takes on new meaning.

Life is brief. Eternity is forever. Keep the wonder of Christmas every day. As the Holy Spirit works in us, the life of Jesus is seen in others, in us. The work that God started continues each day until Jesus comes again.

Because of the loving grace of God, joy is evident in our lives. The presence of a joyful family is the best Christmas gift. From a tiny spark, a mighty flame bursts out to warm the whole room. Christmas is the kindling for new fires. It brings an inner glow. It is lighting a fire inside the soul. The nicest wrapping of all is the loving family who are wrapped up in each other.

For all those who read this book, I pray for a creative season of entering the wonder of waiting and the wonder of God's breaking into our world in the coming of Jesus the Christ.

God did not come to earth to stress us out. God did not give grace so we could wallow in too much traffic, cursing the idiot who did not take advantage of the yellow light so we could make it on time to have lunch downtown with someone you do not think you are able to say no.

Think about your memories of past Christmases to teach how to cherish the present Christmas. Enjoy these things in the present moment. Cherish today. The present time holds a wealth of memories for tomorrow.

Think about the joy of sharing your most valuable possession—time. Stop to listen to a friend rather then rushing away.

A person can close off the senses to many things. To choose to close them to Christmas is to close off oneself to joy.

Chapter Nine
Grace as Hope

Hope looks to the grace of God. Hope is a feeling of expectation or the desire for something. Hope believes. Hope has sure and certain faith in the grace of God. We have experienced crushed hope. We hope for a job or a ministry, but we do not find it. We hope to buy a home. We hope to be graced with children.

Read this book often when a fresh infusion hope is needed. Hope is looking between the bleak places toward the spiritual spaces giving hope and light. Hope is possible no matter what your adverse circumstances.

Blessings of soulful hope teaches us to cling to hope when we cannot see beyond our lives, our work, our homes.

Grace brings hope and safety. Everybody needs hope in dangerous times. Grace is our effective lifeguard. Grace places the soul into Christ as a bee is safe in the hive. Hope is as important to us as water is to a fish. Hope is a wonderful gift, a source of strength to see the light at the end of the tunnel.

The cup of God is brimming with mercy and strength when ours are weak. This hope keeps us humble. Grace renews our faith. We shall soar in the storms like eagles. Grace forgives and forgets our sins. God's cup is brimming with compassion and favor as God sent Jesus to be our personal Savior.

Hope lifts spirits when we become discouraged. Hope reminds us that God is in control when we fear the worst. Hope keeps us going when we feel the worst. Hope fills our recovery when we endure the consequences of bad decisions. Listen to the longing to be free. Allow the wild beauty of the invisible world to gather and embrace grace.

Nothing helps like hope. Fledging writers hope to get published. Married couples hope that their will never be divorce or death. Without a spark of hope, we are doomed to a dark existence. We become fretful, anxious, and droopy as we wait, slowly coming alive to hope. Hope enables us to embrace change. Life becomes bland with no change. We ache for any joyful surprise.

Hope is essential when we fail. Flashbacks of our failures haunt us. The only source for relief is the grace of God. God has given us a purpose for our existence, a reason to go on. Our existence includes tough times. God gives grace to match our trials. God assures us that we are not alone. Light comes after a rain. Failure casts the light despite the initial darkness into a much deeper kindness.

Being alive brings joy. Sense the beauty of being here. Being exiled from our feelings is lonely. Grace is a force that has independence. God is not a lonely divine object. Never forget that every jolt in our rugged journey from earth to heaven reminds us that we are traveling on the right road.

Grace prepares us for glory. God first cleanses us with grace. God then pours in the wine of glory.

The silver link of grace draws the golden link of glory. Grace is glory in a flower bud. Glory is grace in the full flower.

Temporal things may bring pleasure for a season, but grace has eternity in it. Grace is the blossom of eternity. Read I John 2.15-17.

The pull of the world is as strong as gravity. It is relentless, invisible, yet irresistible. With the pride and pleasures of the cosmos so seductive, how can we run the race without being disqualified? Grace shows us the joy of kindness, genuine love prompted by forgiveness. Read Psalm 103:1-5, 11-14.

Grace stretches us into a renewed shape. We received a new self-image. We rise above our fears. Hope is an unstoppable fire. It is fueled by faith. Unquenchable. Unlimited. Blazing in our souls.

Our hope in grace involves our waiting where manna falls. We can expect the dew of the Holy Spirit to fall with the manna.

The graceful power of God goes along with God's word. Hope brings a hint of color on our colorless landscape.

Grace is abiding. We might lose friends, estates, and even life itself, but we will never lose grace. Jewelers have ways to try precious stone. Let us try our grace by a biblical touchstone.

Not everything we hope for will ever happen. Grace may have saved us if we got the job, married the blue eyed blonde, succeeded in doing the will of God. Hope is an anchor for the soul. Read Hebrews 6:19. Hope keeps us steady.

Hope brings a faintly scented perfume. The smell gets stronger he more we remember and recapture it. Hope stirs inside.

Hope is anchored in the grace of God. Breaking an unhealthy habit, losing weight, or accomplishing a task needs encouragement and help.

Millions of people feel helpless. They see no hope for the future. They have no hope of changing.

They have been disappointed in everything. Hopeless causes them to give up on life. They often ask others how they can be so filled with joy and optimism.

Hope is a journey. Peter wrote to the Christians in Asia Minor to have a reason for the hope that was within them. Christians ought to be hopeful. Our hope will show joy, love, boldness, and endurance. Our hope is rooted in the grace of God. Eternal comfort and hope through grace are gifts we receive from God. Our lives are works of grace. God's grace is matchless. Delight in it. Hope in it.

Common grace tells us that God loves everyone. God gives grace to all whether they are aware or not. Saving grace means that God paid the price for anyone who receives the gift of salvation.

Hope also comes with sanctifying grace. God works with us for purification. Read Philippians 1:6. Our hope comes from provisional grace. Read James 1:17. Then there is miraculous grace. This grace happens all the time. Hope also comes in serving grace. God gives each spiritual gifts. Sustaining grace is sufficient grace as Paul accepted. Unmerited favor comes in many forms. God's grace is unlimited.

Paul Tournier wrote that the heart of all churches there are moralistically minded people who want to impose upon others their conditions for salvation. Others live joyously by the marvelous assurance of free salvation. (Paul Tournier, *Guilt and Grace*, p. 195)

When we comprehend the biblical idea of the grace of God, our view of guilt is altered. Paul Tournier, op. cit., p. 170. Grace fulfills the hope of a joyous adventure which is endlessly renewed. God speaks to us in every circumstance. What grace removes in not our guilt, but our condemnation.

In the history of the church, some sects say that converts no longer commit sin. Others major on fear of punishment. Jesus himself spoke about eternal judgement in his parables. Religion can suppress or it can liberate by increasing guilt or removing it. Humans naturally project their guilt upon other people and on God. The fear of being judged is universal and intense. Humans are afraid of each other. Pupils are afraid of teachers. Ministers are afraid of their church members. Fear plays a role in all conflicts. Fearful people do not attack opening up. They continue to brood until conflicts break out in church closings, churches separating from their denominations. Churches and denominations fear each other. They are unconsciously afraid of being convicted of unfaithfulness. All are smirched and none are cleaned.

When and if passions have cooled, reconciliation may be possible. Ungrace people condemn and stew in good faith, with zeal and sincerity. Their vision for ministry is convincing others that their views are in line with the views of God.

Unconscious or repressed guilt seethes with obduracy, aggressiveness, and irritation. Grace produces joy, security, and hope.

We tend to focus on our failures. We need to renew our spirits with the realization that we are a possession of God. God is for us. Joyful thoughts spur us on, remove the guilt, and enjoy the ultimate embrace. That is grace.

"Nothing that is worth doing can be achieved in our lifetime. We must be saved by hope," Reinhold Niebuhr wrote. "Nothing which is true or beautiful or good makes complete sense in any immediate context of history. We must be saved by faith. We are saved by love. No virtuous act is quite as virtuous from the standpoint of our friend or foe. Therefore, we must be saved by the final form of love, which is forgiveness." (Reinhold Niebuhr, The Irony of American History, p. 63)

Chapter Ten
Grace as Beauty

God's beauty and goodness are among the joys that accompanies our awareness of grace. It brings a sensitivity to beauty. Beauty is the language of God. The human eye adores the visible world. For the exploring eye, we fall in love with the abundance of the beautiful.

There is an invisible light that comes when an infant is born. At the other end, the shadows of old age are lit from an invisible world. Taking in the beauty of the visible, we forget that the invisible is a parent of the visible. Now we are seeing through a glass darkly. Grace is harvesting the wisdom of the invisible world.

The image of beauty in our culture is a muscular man or a suntanned, perfectly toned, and swathed in body-hugging clothing. My blonde, blue eyed daughter always enters my mind. I think of the color of hair: the violin playing red head, the athletic brunette, the woman with black hair and overly white smooth skin, and the white-haired nonagenarian. They are comfortable in their own skin with a glamour unique to each one. Each has a gentle spirit and easy smiles.

When I served as a therapist at Lutheran Family Services, counseled many black women. Some of them told me they did not feel attractive. One said, "It's the blue-eyed blondes that are valued as beautiful." As our sessions went on, I use my guidance to help her see how beautiful any race of women can be. I helped her conceive of herself as beautiful. That raised her self-esteem, allowed her to find her charm, and her uniqueness as a woman. She was more radiant each week. After more than 20 years have passed, she sent me an email thanking me for helping her and her family to find joy.

Men as well as women have a feminine relationship with God.

Our souls are not taken by force. Beautiful souls fall in love and receive grace. We begin to look closely at everything. We sense the voice whispering to us. Everywhere we look, God is sending coded messages.

We appreciate all that is alluring, innocent, elegant, and graceful. The world's idea of beauty is an image for our comparison that can never be achieved in life. Women and men age physically. They envision spending beauty dollars to renew their bodies. We have better things to do with our time and money. God abides in our inner most being. God speaks through the delicate human loveliness of body which has become part of your identity. Read Proverbs 31:30.

Our interior lives deepen with time. As we receive the grace of God, we empty ourselves. The rewards are fantastic. God's love is a bounty of endless surprises. God continues to draw us closer. The world might ignore us. We are never less precious to God who never changes. God is the source of beauty; the gift of our interior beauty increases as we continue the process of letting go of the world and embracing the sweetness of grace. God's power speaks through the dramas all around us in nature, as well in our encounters and human experiences.

Connecting with nature makes heaven just a breath, a touch, or a glance away.

Sunrise in Nebraska brings a soft baby pink flanked by translucent clouds of puffy air drifting over Elmwood Park and over the Christian Church located at eye level from our breakfast room. Some days we see fog and mist floating along. Moments of beauty are such delights.

The beauty of the natural world reminds us of the presence of God. Simple things like sunbeams streaming in the windows of our home, walking in the local park opens our hearts to God. God is all around us, conversing with us. By leaning into the everlasting love, our souls receive an unmistakable boost that reverberates through our lives, the lives of others, and on to eternal life.

A soul in love with God is attractive to others. Men sense the guidance of God in retrospect. I look back on my life and see the lost job, amazing opportunities that I missed, illnesses and injuries. Only now, as many years in time have passed, am I able to evaluate my choices.

Laurel my wife and soulmate feels God's presence every day. She has strong feminine gifts like effective intuition and receptivity. God has given her a language of love. What she shares increases joy in others. She is always passionate and joyful as a nurse, as a musician, as a mother and grandma, and as a wife. She is elegantly put together with healthy vitality. As a teenager, she was selected as a beauty queen in midwestern beauty contests. I feel blessed to have a certain standing in her life.

When my beautiful wife and I look at our wrinkles and sagging skin, we realize the impermanence of life on earth that makes way for the eternal beauty. Even thinning bones and lack of muscle strength show that the bodies of beautiful young men and women carved in statues and in Roman and Greek art are frozen in time.

Emperors and kings have statues of themselves out in public eye to make the temporary permanent. Not many statues are created with the bodies of older people. Mature people accept feelings of invisibility that come with age in a culture that discards most everything about those still living at ripe old ages.

Now that I am graced with my wisdom years, I face the challenges of a changing world. I want to be a curator of beauty bringing joy when things are so dark.

Beauty is the gateway to truth. Truth is the gateway to beauty. God is the summit and source of both beauty and truth. Beauty that we can hear, see, and touch leads to a greater loveliness that is divine. Our intuition guides us.

Grace is more than a blue-eyed blonde. Grace is the unconditional offering of God's love. Grace is with us when we least expect it. It is easy to love people when they love you back.

My grandson has a loving dog named Banjo that Ethan and his family rescued. After he was lost, picked up and taken to the shelter, the family brought him home.

Once we have found joy and beauty within, the entire world is infused with beauty. The evidence of grace is always present. Encounters with others are not random occurrences. The beauty of grace is that we are magnificent souls being shaped and molded by sacred and loving hands.

Aging feels like a series of unpleasant surprises. Obsessing about the loss of superficial beauty is a waste of time. Cling to God's timeless presence as true beauty bears radiant fruit throughout life's journey. Real beauty is inside, and it shows when our outer beauty fades.

The process of spiritual awareness is a lifelong journey. The pathway is overwhelming. Grace leads us down our own roads with no predetermined destination. We experience life on a deeper level. We find joy in simple things and in unexpected places.

Our culture elevates beauty, and we are at risk for distraction, even deception. Jesus came into the world wearing swaddling clothes. The community of joy is known for a different kind of beauty. It begins with humility, and it ends in glory. Sharing in the ministry of Jesus in humility brings us to be invited to feast in splendor at the table of grace.

When we stay humble and curious about opportunities to soak up graces and to be more radiant with each passing year, as we use the gift of free will. As we make our own choices, God steps in again and again to bring blessing out of mistakes. Read Romans 8:28. God takes everything we give and turns it in to something beautiful.

Lean back into the arms of grace. Feel the joy of connection. The joy comes in the beauty of silence to stop the ramblings of my mind. "Be still."

Feel a stronger connection to all living things. We are graced by divinity in all things. The beauty of this interconnectedness shows itself in differing ways.

Grace turns up the volume of all our senses. Joy is found in the milieu of each day. Stop now and pray, "Dear God, please allow me to touch at least one person today."

By investing your time and energy, grace becomes a more tangible part of life. Graceful acts build strong, intimate bonds with others.

Generations to come will be influenced by this grace.

I add to my prayer list the people I meet over my days of living. Prayer makes a difference. Living in the fruit of the Spirit depends on our intimate communication.

When I preached in my home church, Woodlawn Baptist Church in Bristol, Tennessee, one worship song was about remembering people who helped us into heaven. When our souls finally enter heaven, a huge army of people who were blessed by God's grace through some simple act of kindness, including our faithful and intimate prayers, will be waiting to welcome us.

While souls are being sanctified to enter heaven, they can expect both joys and sorrows as they anticipate eternal joy.

There is beauty in our imperfection and brokenness. We home in on our flaws. Following the realities of living, the pain, shame, and disappointments, we embrace the imperfection and brokenness we all experience. Grace is seeing it all as beauty. Soul renewal and hope causes us not to be so sad in our brokenness. Broken places are grace entrances.

A broken life becomes broken open by God's love. Life becomes more radiant in God's light. A glimmer of hope opens our bounded souls. Hope floods us with love, more than enough fire to thaw our cold souls.

We embrace our shredded past. We look between the gaps, and we are made whole again. In those gaps in-between spaces and breathing places, we perceive beyond what is in front. We discern spiritual truth clearer than before through the lens of grace.

Living in divine love is the only answer to our human longings. In the image and likeness of God, our loving fills us. We are created for love and intimacy; everybody longs for love. God engages each of us, in every phase of life, in conversation overflowing with grace and love. Blessed be the longing that brought us here in the quickening of wonder. Be aware that life is a mystery. Liveliness emerges at dusk and dawn when our souls rise higher, and we are grateful to be born.

The notion of desire brings beauty. We are children of the desire of our parents for each other. We are creatures of desire because we are creations of desire. Some beautiful things happen to us in solitude. We want to know what is original. We must leave the expected perceptions that manipulate our experiences. The writing life is vulnerable. It is an overwhelming place. It is expressed in restlessness. Souls long for the eternal. The eye of beauty glimpses possibility.

We can trust God to bring good out of every moment. We have a taste for mystery as we test the unknown. When we are open to the healing light, God pours it on, empowering and transforming our lives for the better. Cultivating gratitude paves the soul to be sensitive to beauty.

Within our darkened days, there lies hidden joy waiting to surprise us. As we maintain a lively imagination that we had in childhood, we encounter fresh realities.

Counting our blessing every day resurrects joy and puts all our perceived inadequacies in perspective. Read Psalm 139:13-14. Each day is not the same. Nobody remains changeless. Days move forward in moments. Once a moment flickers into life, it vanishes and is replaced.

That is why we celebrate. That is why we must never become so enamored by the substitutions sought in this culture that we forget or ignore.

Those spending their time and energy on the writing life go to the computer to meet the empty page. She has no idea what will come out. She desires to rise above her circumstances to experience hope, even before there is clear and unmistakable evidence yet.

We mirror earth's ability to wait patiently to prepare for fresh rising and growth. We gain a fresh awareness of how faith and grace entwine and how much creation and its beauty must

teach us about pausing and beginning again. Hope arises inside us as we learn to observe the signposts of shifting and change not only in earth's cycles. That is the beauty of grace.

Bibliography

Baines, Edward, *The Works of Isaac Watts, D.D. in Seven Volumes*. Leeds, England: Henry Fish Printers, 1800.

Baird, David. *Christmas: Decorations, Feasts, Gifts, and Traditions*. London: MQ Publications, 2007.

Barber, Benjamin. *Consumed: How Markets Corrupt Children, Infantilize Adults, and Swallow Citizens Whole*. New York: W.W. Norton Books, 2009.

Barber, Michael Patrick. *The True Meaning of Christmas: The Birth of Jesus and the Origins of the Season*. Greenwood Village, Colorado: Augustine Institute Press, 2021.

Bass, Dorothy and Mark R. Schwehm. *Leading Lives That Matter: What We Should Do and Who We Should Be*. Grand Rapids, Michigan: Eerdmans and Company, 2009.

Brooks, David. *The Road to Character*. New York: Penguin Random Hose, 2015.

Bridges, Jerry. *Pursuit of Holiness*. Grand Rapids, Michigan: Eerdmans Publishers, 2014.

Forest, Jim. *All Is Grace: A Biography of Dorothy Day*. New York: Orbus Press, 2011.

Frykholm, Amy, "The Five Spiritual Senses, Christianity Today", November 17, 2021, pp. 23-25.

Job, Rueben. *A Guide to Spiritual Discernment*. Nashville: Upper Room Books, 1996.

Johnson, Robert. *Balancing Heaven and Earth: A Memoir of Visions, Dreams, and Realizations*. San Francisco: Harper and Sons, 1998.

Lamott, Ann. *Bird by Bird: Some Instructions on Writing and Life*. New York: Anchor Books, 1995.

Law Eric. *Inclusion: Making Room for Grace*. Saint Louis: Chalice Press, 2000.

Niebuhr, Reinhold. *The Irony of American History*. Chicago: University of Chicago Press, 2009.

Oden, Marilyn Brown. *Abundance: Joyful Living in Christ*. *Nashville*: Upper Room Books, 2004.

O'Donohue, John. *Beauty, the Invisible Embrace: Rediscovering the True Sources of Compassion, Serenity, and Hope*. New York: Harper Perennial Books, 2008.

Peterson, Eugene. *God's Message of Christmas Love*. Nashville: Countryman, a division of Thomas Nelson, 2005.

Peterson, Eugene. *The Message: The New Testament in Contemporary English*. Colorado Springs: Navpress, 1993.

Rohr, Richard. *Preparing for Christmas*. Cincinnati: Franciscan Publishers, 2010.

Rohr, Richard. *Simplicity*. New York: Crossroad Publishing Company, 2003.

Stimpson, Emily. *These Beautiful Bones: An Everyday Theology of the Body*. Steubenville, Ohio: Emmaus Road Press, 2014.

Tillich, Paul. *The Essential Tillich*. New York: Scribner, 1999.

Tournier, Paul. *Guilt and Grace*. New York: Harper and Row, 1962.

Tournier, Paul. *The Person Reborn*. New York: Harper and Row, 1966.

Williamson, Marianne. *Everyday Grace: Having Hopes, Finding Forgiveness, and Making Miracles*. Houston: Riverhead Books, 2022.

Yancey, Philip. *What's So Amazing Abut Grace?* Grand Rapids, Michigan: Zondervan Publishing House, 1997.

About the Author

Preacher, pastor, author Dr. James McReynolds has been graced as one who has been raised up from poverty and a culture of needed grace. During his School of Practical Christianity in New York, Norman Vincent Peale graced him with the joy of oil, anointing him the Minister of Joy to the World.

Born in Kingsport, Tennessee, he had a humble beginning. His family lived in a small one-room apartment. His poor parents were quite young. The joy of the Lord has been his strength given by grace. He was the first person in his family to attend college.

During 2023, he will celebrate his Platinum Jubilee with 70 years as an ordained minister. Jim has devoted his life to teaching the world how to create an atmosphere of grace that has revolutionized lives of countless people.

He has been graced to use his gifts for the Sunday School Board of the Southern Baptist Convention, the largest Protestant denomination in the world. He was graced to serve as moderator for the Nebraska region of the Christian Church (Disciples of Christ) in the United States and Canada.

Jim has been given commendation in numerous places with awards from many sources including honorary degrees, grants for study, and the honor of being an elite member as an admiral in the Nebraska Navy by decree of the governor of the state.

There is no ocean in Nebraska, but McReynolds has crossed the world's oceans multiple times. He has been graced by God to earn nine academic degrees including five doctorates. His books bring fresh air to the church.

Jim's focus is on the grace of God whose joy eclipses all else. The beauty of God's grace converts souls in the years God chose him for gracing places, life environments, and for eternal ministry that never ends. The multitude of books he has written on joy and life in the kingdom are filled with the joy of what God is doing by divine grace.

Surrendering to the Spirit, to the grace of preaching, writing, and teaching is the way God uses us and all our gifts to humbly realize our small place as servants of the kingdom.

For the many people who have given up on the church, his fresh air enables them to breathe with grace. He has experienced decades of vulnerable ministry in the local congregation and in churches throughout the world. His time on earth has created an apologetic for joy as the gift to inspire and renew.

As you read this book or hear Jim preach, you will discover that the joy God graces us with are more satisfying than we could ever imagine.